THE UNAUTHORIZED

D A I L Y
MEDITATION
M A N U A L

Like the man said, "The only thing we have to fear is fear itself."

ENSIGN KIM : THE THAW: Stardate Not Given

There is some debate whether "the man" Kim refers to was Franklin Roosevelt, the pre-Federation leader who presided over one of Terra's most serious economic depressions—or whether he meant Ru'agh KoHbar, an even earlier Klingon leader who inspired his fellow warriors to repel a vastly superior Romulan invasion force.

It hardly matters. Thousands of leaders from hundreds of planets have made virtually the same statement, many of them recorded millenia before either Terra or Qo'noS *had* any written records. Because the fact is, fear is an almost universal experience. And although it is as irrational as it is universal, it follows certain identifiable "laws".

One of those laws is that fear feeds on itself. Our original fear is rarely the culprit. How easily we let it grow, how often we seek out other people with the same fear so we might "justify" our own; and then how others' fears end up doubling and re-doubling our own until a kind of mass panic sets in—*those* are the real culprits.

Another "law" is that this panic is almost unstoppable until it "runs its course". Which simply means that the best counter-measure is not to let it happen in the first place.

That which creates our fear is not the enemy. *Fear* is.

I confront my fears as soon as I sense them. While accepting their role in signaling potential problems, I will make sure fear itself isn't one of them.

SECTOR

CORRESPONDING TO THE TERRAN MONTH OF
November

You might as well sit back and enjoy the ride.

CAPTAIN KIRK: METAMORPHOSIS: 3219.4

We are strengthened by struggle. We grow through facing life's challenges, hooking up with new resources, and working to change our conditions for the better.

But some conditions *can't* be changed. Some things that happen simply can't be controlled. The only thing we *can* change in these cases is our attitude about them. The only thing we can control is *how we react.*

An Arabic parable is told about a farmer who can't seem to rid his garden of weeds. Finally he travels to the Caliph's palace—several days by camel—to seek the advice of the royal gardener. The wizened gardener listens, then offers several suggestions. The farmer thanks him, goes home and tries each suggestion... without success. He thereupon returns to the palace to complain that he has tried everything, and still he has weeds.

The royal gardener scowls, thinks for some minutes more. "There is one last thing you can try on your weeds," he says at last. "You can learn to love them."

When we can't rid our gardens of the weeds, when the voyage is underway and there's no stopping now, we can still make a choice. We can decide to accept the experience, and then extract whatever goodness and growth The Universe has prepared for us.

I will seek to change what I am able, find good-ness in the rest, and trust The Universe to care for me no matter how bumpy the ride.

11.2

Spare me the analysis. It's enough that it works!

DR. McCOY: MIRI: 2713.5

Sometimes asking how or why is the *worst* thing we can do. Sometimes *not* understanding is what "works".

The rational mind is a wonderful thing. Few people would give back their intellect for the unreflective, half-conscious existence of some primordial Garden of Eden. And yet, in harvesting the fruits of the Tree of Knowledge, our minds *do* occasionally get in our own way.

Most of our body's life-preserving mechanisms evolved long before rational thought—and still work best without it. Healing from illness, for example, is a natural process we can short-circuit if we over-analyze or worry about it. Not that we can't use mental affirmations and medical technologies. It's our egotistical need to "control" the process that becomes a problem. If we would only *accept* our healing, we would improve our recovery.

Our emotional and spiritual lives operate in much the same way. If we learn to *trust* our inner resources, to celebrate and strengthen our connection to our Source, we will receive the guidance and healing we seek.

"Let go and let God" is a traditional way to put it. It's the difference between praying for what *we think* we need, and attuning oneself to a Universe that *already knows.*

I accept my inner, subconscious resources as well as my intellect. I will seek a balance that works for me, and embrace opportunities to test it.

Mistakes? I have made some fine ones.

CAPTAIN PICARD : JUSTICE : 41255.6

The universal slogan, "Nobody's perfect," was never meant to excuse bad behavior, or to absolve us from the continuing goal of personal and communal redemption. (Or, if you prefer, "self-improvement".) Indeed, redemption applies *only* to the ongoing refinement of that which is *im*perfect.

Ironically, our imperfections are the required first steps toward improvement. It's not just that getting it wrong *precedes* getting it right. That's what *helps* us get it right.

Like Captain Picard, the most inspiring models in Starfleet history did not breeze through The Academy—or go on to serve The Federation—with unblemished records. The same with *human* history. The most beloved Holy Ones were cherished as much for their raw humanity as their "divinity". Even the paradigm Avatars and Incarnations had their moments of blind rage, their dark nights of doubt, their strategic blunders… their imperfections.

And the reason we continue to draw inspiration from these models is precisely because they *were* so imperfect; because they were as fully "human" as *we* are; because they were subject to the same flaws and temptations of living "in the flesh"—and yet they kept going, kept trying, kept growing. And if *they* could, so can *we*.

I will not condone my mistakes simply because others have made them. Others learn *from them, transcend them. I choose to follow their example.*

11.4

You can't snatch people and put them into your fantasies and expect them to respond.

COMMANDER RIKER : TRUE Q : 46192.3

Back in Terra's early days of imaging technology, there was a thriving religious subculture whose members refused to allow "photographs" to be taken of them. The Amish (as they are still known) were therefore regarded as a bit "quaint". Maybe they were just being careful.

Not because they thought the images contained some sort of magic, like the voodoo dolls that could reportedly be used to "control" the people they resembled. It's just that photographs were such superficial copies of people. They couldn't capture a person's true identity; they couldn't speak for themselves. Or *defend* themselves.

Which tempted whoever possessed the photograph to read any personality into the picture they might want. That fantasy would then become attached to the visual image. And *that* would inevitably affect their expectations and reactions to the *real* person if they should ever meet.

Our fantasies about other people operate in the same way. We become boxed in by our "images" and private thoughts about others, rather than letting their behavior and interactions *with us* define who they are.

People need freedom to be themselves, to grow toward their *own* vision, not ours. If we give them that freedom, we have all the more right to expect it for ourselves.

I am not bound by others' fantasies. I am who my thoughts, intentions and actions reveal me to be.

Who am I to argue with me?

DR. BASHIR : VISIONARY : Stardate Not Given

"Conflicted". It describes the psychological state when one part of us says "yes", another part "no". It's the painful condition of having an idea of where we want to be, while realizing how far we have to go before we get there.

In Bashir's statement, "I" is the self we *can be,* and "me" is the person we *are.* All too often, *who we are* dominates the argument. Which means we effectively stop growing. Our present identity, with all its weaknesses and self-enforced boundaries, remains in control.

But the very fact of internal conflict is actually a good sign. Conflict confirms that we stand at the threshold of change, and it's only natural to experience resistance from an ego which fears being replaced.

The Vulcan approach can help us here—first, by simply reminding us that our egos are not our *selves.* Who We Are is a transitory phenomenon, a work-in-progress. And if we look at that "work" without emotion, without attachment, we can begin to decide what kind of person we'd like to be... and then make the logical choices that bring us more and more into alignment with that vision.

Who am I to argue with me—? "Me" considers it an argument. "I" understands that it's really a healthy discussion about realizing our potential.

It is natural to experience inner conflict. I trust the Path I have embarked on to guide me through conflict to higher awareness, and to my higher Self.

11.6

When your only reality is an illusion, then illusion is a reality.

THE CLOWN: THE THAW: Stardate Not Given

It's remarkable how "reality" is defined by our initial experiences. People who grow up in poverty or fear or conflict think *that's* what life is all about. Space travelers who have crashed on uncharted planets, who have been forced to start over without the benefits of their previous technology, have raised new generations that seem to accommodate themselves to hardship as if that condition is the normal routine. Having experienced nothing else, that is their reality. It's also an illusion.

The truth is, *all* of our personal experiences of what's routine, or normal, or "what life is all about", are only a tiny bandwidth in an incomprehensibly larger spectrum.

Which is why we cannot depend on only our own eyes. However comfortable we may be with our local version of reality, we must look beyond that limited horizon to have any sense of what the greater Reality is. We must talk to other people, read books about other people's lives, past and present, around the globe and across the galaxy.

The immediate benefit is not simply an expansion of our reality, but expanded possibilities, more options, a deeper, boader, more inter-connected sense of Self.

And inevitably, one by one, our illusions disappear.

I am overcoming my illusions. Each week I will give myself one new experience. And I will ask some-one from a different culture about their experience.

We're going to get through this together!

KES: PHAGE: 48532.4

Virtually no sentient species has yet been discovered—from one end of the galaxy to the other—whose evolutionary origins designed it for a totally isolated existence. Certain individuals within a species may become accustomed to being alone; a few may even come to prefer it. But their biological make-up practically *shouts* for companionship.

We are, in other words, hard-wired for community.

This is no more evident than in periods of great turmoil or personal distress. Even our apparent instinct to withdraw at such times, to "be by ourselves", is a call to be "missed" by someone, a reaching out to be rescued from conditions that feel like they're picking on us alone.

Except that we are never truly "alone". And we must not allow anyone *else* to be alone for long. Because study after study has shown how social isolation destroys individuals—and eventually destroys the societies that continue to allow those individuals' wounds to fester. Whether the wounds are real or imagined.

Our personal and communal destinies are as intertwined as the nerves in our brains. There is nothing we can't "get through" if we act accordingly. And few things we can't achieve if we do it together.

My consolation, my strength, comes from reaching out to others—to give help as much as receive it.

11.8

When we do battle, it is only because we have no choice.

CAPTAIN KIRK: THE SQUIRE OF GOTHOS: 2124.5

Virtually without exception, people who go out looking for a fight are really at war with themselves. "Enemies" only reflect the personal demons they are still battling.

But even when we've overcome our aggressive tendencies, open conflict with others can sometimes seem unavoidable. Or even the *right* thing to do.

Kirk's fellow crewmembers knew better. "War is never imperative," Dr. McCoy reminds us. "There are always alternatives," Spock would add, raising an eyebrow.

And there *are*. So is Captain Kirk mistaken?

Not if we read between the lines. When we resort to violence—personally or communally—it's not because we *have* no choice. It's because we *think* we have no choice.

Maybe we think we're alone. Or we think no one else can (or *will*) intervene. Or we're so emotionally close to the situation that we can't think straight to begin with.

But that only goes to show how much we need others to point out what we often can't see ourselves. We need a network of people—the more diverse the better—who may have been down this path before; who can help both sides visualize the consequences. And who, together, can keep the peace long enough to let us work things out.

"I have no choice" is a statement of perspective, not fact. I can always call on others, and on my own inner light, to help change my perspective.

There are times when it's best just to let things out.

COUNSELOR TROI: PARALLELS: 47391.2

Much has already been said about our bodies' needs—about the importance of keeping in touch with the physical/emotional legacy we've inherited from our species' evolution. And the fact is, if we don't continually work on integrating body and mind, we risk *dis*-integration. Or, in the medical jargon of past centuries, schizophrenia.

Of course, there are layers of social conventions concerning the "proper" expression of physical and emotional urges, as well as sound reasons for *not* expressing them. We learn to control our anger because it might destroy crucial relationships. We restrain our sexual instincts because unchecked reproduction now works *against* our species' survival. We also choke back tears; we stifle our laughter; and we try to hide how frightened we really are.

And the toll can be devastating. Because the psychic energy of all those repressed emotions doesn't just go away. It builds like water behind a dam. Finding ways to rechannel that energy—art, perhaps, or athletics—is essential. But sometimes the best solution is simply to find a "safe haven" where those emotions can be expressed in their most primitive form: To cry in sorrow, pound our fists in anger, and shout for joy. Because dams break.

It is healthy and natural to release my emotions. I will find a private place, or relationship, or group, where I can do so safely, and in mutual trust.

11.10

Curious how my failure, added to your own, should improve your feelings.

LIEUTENANT TUVOK: STATE OF FLUX: 48568.2

It *is* curious. Most of us are so conscious of our own faults and mistakes that we find great reassurance in the faults and mistakes of others. It's a healthy response if it prevents us from being too harsh on ourselves, if it frees us to make the mistakes that precede genuine growth.

But there's a danger: This kind of "reassurance" can easily develop into "delight". And then we start *looking* for faults and weaknesses in others—especially in our competitors, or even our leaders. We begin to revel in scandal, calling out the media bloodhounds to dig up more for us, to spell out everything they find in lurid detail.

Why? Because it serves to further excuse our *own* weakness. Because if we concentrate on others' defects we can ignore our own. *And* we can continue to avoid the self-transformation that, deep down, we already know is needed but our egos hope to delay as long as possible.

We need to counter this mindset. Not so much by turning a deaf ear to the latest gossip, or by deciding not to download the latest edition of *Galactic Enquirer*. The solution is to revel in our achievements for a change, to focus on the *good* things we find in each other.

And what's *really* curious is that we'll not only improve our feelings, we'll improve our *lives*.

I will look upon others' faults as a reminder to work on my own. I will find something good in everyone.

The more we fight each other, the weaker we'll get and the less chance we'll have.

COMMANDER SISKO: THE WAY OF THE WARRIOR: 49011.4

One hallmark of our progress along the Spiritual Path is how well we've overcome our inbred violence.

The biological roots of violence are strong in most sentient species, and usually stronger in one sex. The urge to inflict harm is literally a primitive one, connected with our emergence from the animal kingdom. It was the inevitable outcome of our competition for territory, for reproductive dominance, for self-preservation.

But it almost never meant death. Violence was the painful, pre-sentient, pre-verbal message to go find another valley to live in, or another mate to live with—or at least to submit to someone else's rules about where and with whom to live. Killing was rarely necessary to make the point. And still *is* for most non-sentient species.

Ironic that this same non-lethal violence, now combined with our technological "progress", has turned us into killers. It has also brought mass destruction of property and endless arms races, not to mention the stealing of precious resources from other, more peaceful uses.

As citizens of the universe, our progress depends on fighting *this legacy*, not each other. Fortunately, if we recognize our weakness, we can make it our strength.

Within me are echoes of the distant past. To go on living in the present, I must transcend the past by affirming the person I wish to become in the future.

11.12

The logical course is not always the right course.

COMMANDER CHAKOTAY : TATTOO : Stardate Not Given

Once again: Logic has its place. But like a computer, it still needs an operator. Most of all, it needs good data.

Suppose we ask the Ship's Computer to plot the most direct course to a distant star system. Unfortunately, we fail to tell it that a massive black hole lies somewhere between here and there. Or maybe we don't even *know* about the black hole. Chances are, our Starship will end up a few light years off-course due to gravitational effects we didn't account for—assuming our logically-plotted route hasn't already drilled us into the black hole itself!

Our lives are much the same. There are so many variables that may affect our course, some we don't even *know* about. We can certainly use our logic to guide us when enough data is available. But we must also polish the skills that help us fly by the seat of our pants.

One of these, as Chakotay knows, is intuition. Whether we picture this inner guidance system as "animal guides" or Higher Self or Spirit, all of us have a course-correcting ability that is beyond logic, beyond conscious thought.

At this deeper level, the right course for us is already laid in. We have only to listen for its guidance. In fact, learning to listen is part of the "course".

I can know what the right course is for me. As I learn to "listen" through daily meditation, I can also know when changes in direction are necessary.

Our job is not to police the galaxy.

COMMANDER RIKER: LOUD AS A WHISPER: 42477.2

The policies of governments begin with individuals. People tend to translate what they believe privately, what works in their own personal lives, to the public level.

It's possible, therefore, to read Riker's words not so much as a statement about Federation policy as a warning to each of us *personally.*

Because all too often we *do* take the role of policeman. We monitor what others are doing, who their friends are. We make judgments. And sometimes we intervene by offering advice, or helping to solve problems—or even by forcing our lifestyle and standards on others.

Such "help" is rarely appreciated, and may even create an atmosphere of resentment or rebellion. Especially if it's ongoing. Or if it stifles others' freedom to make mistakes, to develop their capacity to think for themselves.

Our "job" is to police our *own* lives. In fact, if we find ourselves meddling in other peoples' lives, it's probably because we haven't been policing our own properly. Often, the only way our subconscious can show us the flaws we still need to fix in ourselves is *through others.*

So let's concentrate on cleaning up our own house first. Then, by our example, we'll have far more influence on others than we'd ever have by flashing a badge.

I am responsible for prescribing, and living up to, my own standards. My success in that effort is what translates into a positive influence on others.

11.14

I have a human half you see as well as an alien half... constantly at war with each other. I survive it because my intelligence wins out, makes them live together.

SPOCK: THE ENEMY WITHIN: 1673.5

Inner conflict is hardly a new subject on these pages. Or in our personal lives. All of us feel the occasional warring of factions within us—between our intellect and our emotions, for example. Or between desire and duty.

Another subject that's not exactly new is the need for some kind of mediating force to make our warring factions "live together." For Spock, the mediator was his intelligence. For most of us, however, that isn't enough.

...Unless, perhaps, we capitalize the word.

Because "Intelligence" happens to be another name for the greater power that *is* enough—to do anything.

It is not necessary to worship that Intelligence the way our ancestors carried on with in their gods. We have only to recognize that the Power sustaining the universe also sustains *us*. The Law which balances a star's exploding interior with its own gravitational collapse—and in the process creates light—can also balance the thoughts and feelings which sometimes explode inside *us*.

Our inner conflict is actually a sign of this Intelligence. We can be sure its ultimate purpose is to create light.

The Intelligence reflected in the universe is also at work within me. Through my inner conflict I become aware of the lessons it is trying to teach me.

Sometimes the bad memories can be the most intense of all.

ENGINEER LA FORGE : VIOLATIONS : 45429.3

If we admit that Geordi's observation is true, *why* is it true? Why should unpleasant memories be stronger?

First, let's be clear about what *isn't* the correct explanation: The intensity of bad memories is *not* meant as punishment. It is *not* designed to induce guilt. And its purpose is *not* to make us feel bad about ourselves, or our "worthiness" to feel joy and fulfillment.

The fact is, in the language of emotion, intensity is almost always a function of *importance*.

If we feel especially bad about something we did, our subconscious is telling us that there is an important lesson to be gained from the experience; and chances are we haven't learned it yet. If we are unusually disturbed by a past event—sometimes even if we weren't directly involved—our body/mind is sending us a signal that there is special significance in that event for us; and we still need to come to grips with some issue it has raised.

Our memories have a practical function, of course. But our feelings about them are meant to teach us, to make us wiser, and ultimately to bring us into a more productive relationship with other people and the universe.

Even my bad memories are for my own good. I will reflect on those that hurt most, and with the help of others learn the lessons hiding within them.

11.16

I'm sure I could be more productive if I didn't have to regenerate every day.

ODO: FOR THE CAUSE: Stardate Not Given

If only we didn't need sleep! If only we could *use* that extra seven or eight hours a day (Humans/Bajorans), or three hours (Vulcans/Klingons); then we would get so much more done! Or at least have more time to enjoy life.

Or would we—? Because even though Odo is restating a complaint we *all* have (in his own terms, of course), his characteristic sarcasm betrays a recognition that regenerating (or sleeping) isn't just an annoying necessity. It's actually the best use of those precious hours.

After all, it's not as if *nothing* is going on. Like the Ship's Computer shutting down to optimize its data-banks and run systems checks, our own "down time" enables us to process our experiences and consolidate learning. No artifical version of this procedure is half as effective.

And not only do we need *daily* "regeneration", our productivity is enhanced even more by weekly breaks and regularly-scheduled shore leave.

It's so easy to get caught up in our duties. And it helps our egos to think no one else could do what we do, so we'd better stay on the job. But if "observing the Sabbath" weren't already carved in sacred stone, we'd be forced to invent the practice for our own good. It's *that* important.

Today I will begin meditating on my next scheduled holiday. I will open myself to entirely new places and possibilities my inner spirit will suggest to me.

...Adopting a siege mentality is ultimately self-defeating.

LT. COMMANDER WORF: TO THE DEATH: Stardate Not Given

Fortify the ramparts. Shut the gates. Batten down the hatches. Here they come again!

According to the siege mentality, it's us against everybody else. Life is a defensive action. KEEP OUT!

Even if it's understandable, it's a bad strategy.

For one thing, building a fence is almost an invitation to have it broken down. Not that destroying someone else's fence is our "right". It's just that people are naturally curious; what do you have that you're hiding? Besides, people are *social* animals; we expect others to interact with us, not build walls of separation and isolation.

What's more, the walls people build to keep others out ultimately *change them*—usually for the worse. Either they become hardened to the rest of the world ("I've got mine, now go get your own"); or they grow increasingly paranoid ("Everyone's trying to take away what I have"). Fortresses breed fear, not a sense of safety.

Our best "defense", it turns out, is to get out *in* the world—to show others who we are, what we believe in, and how we've earned what we have. To show that we are in the world *for* something, not to stand against it.

And the best thing is, The Universe stands behind us when we do that. Which changes us—for the *better*.

My best protection is to simply be Who I Am, without fear, and with respect for Who Others Are.

11.18

This is one puppet who doesn't like her strings pulled.

MAJOR KIRA: VISIONARY: Stardate Not Given

In a sense we *are* puppets. All of us have so-called "heartstrings" that others can tug on to arouse our sympathies. We also have "hot buttons"—sensitive places in our psyches that can trigger anger or jealousy or lust, or cause us to react in other predictable ways.

But most of us don't *like* having our strings pulled or our buttons pushed. We don't appreciate the feeling that we're being "manipulated" by someone else. Worse, we don't like the idea that we *can* be manipulated, that someone could actually bypass our rational minds and play our emotions like a keyboard.

Which is why some of us flatly deny it. Trouble is, that only makes us *more* vulnerable to manipulation. By assuming that no one else can control us, we close our eyes to defenses that might prevent us from *being* controlled. We also fail to accept an important part of who we are.

Ironically, not liking our strings pulled is a crucial step toward transcending our "puppethood". At least we're *aware* of it. Only then can we learn how to prevent it, or how to pull our *own* strings in pursuit of our goals.

We might also learn when The Universe is pulling, and when to just sit back and enjoy the dance.

The fact that I can sometimes be manipulated is no dishonor. I am learning what my "strings" are, and how to use that knowledge to my advantage.

*We are born, we grow, we live, and we die.
In all the ways that matter we are alike.*

CAPTAIN PICARD : WHO WATCHES THE WATCHERS? : 43173.5

So... how fine do you want to cut it?

Admittedly, our ability to make distinctions serves a useful purpose. The minute differences we see in nature give us greater control over it; they increase our species' chances for survival; they enhance our own creativity and sense of personal satisfaction. Our ability *matters*.

But when it comes to inter-personal relationships—to getting along with other races and species—what "matters" then? Should noticing that someone has blue eyes rather than brown make a difference? What about brown skin versus pink? Thinning grey hair or lustrous blonde? Flowing robes or tight-fitting uniforms? Should someone's praying to nature, or to a sacred icon, or to no one at all, automatically determine how we relate to them?

We can make all these distinctions betweeen people, and even finer ones. But which are *necessary?* Which serve a beneficial purpose? Captain Picard may oversimplify to make the point. But the truth is, noticing differences often raises artificial barriers that can harm us.

And the deeper truth is this: If we remain divided from others, we can't be united with ourselves. But, tear down the walls outside, and the divisions within us are healed.

*I can retain my critical powers without letting them
dictate my relationships. Today, if I catch myself
noticing a difference, I will find only the good in it.*

11.20

You choose your enemies, you choose your friends. But family... that's in the stars.

ENGINEER O'BRIEN: THE ICARUS FACTOR: 42686.4

In one sense, O'Brien's claim seems to contradict other advice you'll find in this *Manual*. Haven't we said that each of us defines "family" for ourselves? Isn't our support network, and the spiritual tradition we align ourselves with—which we *choose*—our family too?

Of course. But biology is still at our core. Every species has its "blood relations". Even with genetic engineering, we cannot change our heritage.

Nor should we try. The Universe does not throw us into biological units haphazardly. There is meaning and reason for *this* mother and father, *that* brother or sister, *this* uncle, *that* grandmother. Or the lack of them. For O'Brien, "in the stars" is shorthand for acknowledging just how important these relationships are, not merely in terms of our physical existence, but our spiritual growth.

At some point in our lives, it's not uncommon to wish we could replace this biological unit with another one. But these most intimate relationships, as difficult, confrontational—and yes, even abusive—as they may be, are those we are destined to learn the most from.

By facing both their pain and their joy, we take on a heritage beyond biology, as deep as boundless Spirit.

I accept the family locked into my chromosomes. I unlock my spiritual self by learning the lessons only these relationships can teach me.

Are you doing the best thing... or are you doing what's best for you—?

DR. CRUSHER: BLOODLINES: 47829.1

It's always a good question. At face value it asks us whether our actions are mostly selfish, or if we're taking others into account. If we *are,* are we considering the effects of our actions only on those in our own social circle? Or could there be consequences for the wider community? Or on people we may not even know?

The irony here is that "the best thing" and what's "best for you" are ultimately the same. We only *think* there's a difference because our view is so narrow, or only concerned with the short term. If we would consider all the people we touch, if we could account for the long-term ramifications, we'd see how our own particular interests are virtually inseparable from the best interests of *all.*

The problem is, we can't do that. We're not omnipotent. Nor do we always have the time to analyze these things beforehand. Besides, taking care of our own small patch of the universe really *is* our primary responsibility.

But we *can* draw on other people's advice whenever it's practical. We can also "check in" with The Universe through regular meditation and other spiritual exercises.

Because it's along this Path where the selfish and the self*less* merge. Where what's best is simply *what's best.*

I work toward the goal of making what's "best for me" what's best for those around me. Starting with family and friends, I will continually widen my circle.

11.22

We don't have to like each other to work well together.

COMMANDER RIKER: THE BEST OF BOTH WORLDS, PART II: 44001.4

Most of us do not work—or live—in isolation. In the course of our daily routines we will interact with dozens of other people. And chances are, at least a few of these people will reflect personal qualities we won't like.

Like... Such a misnomer. Because to "like" someone usually means to *be like* them, to see something we have in common. And yet much of what we see in others are the very qualities we *don't* like in ourselves. So we often end up *dis*liking those who are most like us, and liking those whom we are *not* like (but would *like* to be like).

All of which is simply to point out how fickle our "likes" are, how unreliable they are as guides to interpersonal relationships. Some of our planet's greatest advances, after all, have come from partnerships between people who haven't particularly liked one another. Or worse.

But Riker's advice isn't ultimately about learning to work with people even if we don't like them. It's about learning not to make that superficial assessment in the first place. It's about giving them a chance. It's about giving our*selves* a chance to seek out the goodness in others that makes us "like" them, and allowing others to discover the goodness to "like" in us.

I will think of at least one trait I have in common with each person I encounter today. I will look for the things in my co-workers that make us alike.

There's only one kind of woman or man. You either believe in yourself or you don't.

CAPTAIN KIRK: MUDD'S WOMEN: 1329.1

It's like saying a woman is "slightly pregnant". Sorry, pal—either she *is*, or she *isn't*. There is, by definition, no room for qualifiers.

In the same way, an individual can be said to "believe in himself or herself"—or *not*. There is no middle ground.

The question is, *how* do you believe in yourself? Is it a function of self-confidence? Is it about being "right" or "successful" in enough past situations that you can pretty much count on being right or successful in the future?

Hardly. People can believe in themselves even while feeling unsure about the "correctness" of their decisions or the outcome of their actions. In fact, it's their belief that drives them to proceed *despite* all those uncertainties.

It's the belief that life is less about being right or successful than being honest and courageous. It's about being willing to try, to make mistakes, to continually push the boundaries of your experience, to recognize your place in a larger whole and to take responsibility for it.

Finally, it's about saying "Yes!" to your own life.

To believe in yourself is to affirm that life has meaning. Regardless of the outcome. Despite the hardships. And even if you still haven't discovered what that meaning *is*.

I can believe this: That my life is good, even when doubt clouds my vision; that I will endure and grow, in failure as well as success.

11.24

I never fully appreciated how difficult and how rewarding it is to be human.

COUNSELOR TROI: THE LOSS: 44356.9

Just to be in the game is an honor. To be born into this world, to be alive and conscious, is a reward in itself.

Not that life doesn't send us difficulties that can make us wonder if being alive is all that great. What's worse, while we're having all those difficulties we end up fantasizing about how things might have been. But far from comforting us, our dreams of a better life only increase our pain. Our ability to imagine heaven makes our current problems seem all the more like hell.

But let's try imagining *this:* Let's say we were given a choice before entering this world. We could have been incarnated as a happy, contented pig—or the calloused, get-up-at-dawn farmer who feeds it. One has a secure, mud-filled pen and all the corn cobs he can eat. The other has twelve-hour workdays... and the stars at night.

In a sense, we've already made the choice. And we make it again with each new day. We trade an unconscious, unknowing, unmerited contentment for the conscious fulfillment we must *earn* by overcoming countless obstacles and character defects.

To be "human" is to finally appreciate that having to earn it *is* the highest reward.

I am grateful for the challenges in my life. I will reward myself for overcoming them. The Universe will reward me for the stronger person I become.

I suggest that good spirits might make an effective weapon.

SPOCK: DAY OF THE DOVE: Stardate Not Given

When nothing else works, when one of life's sticky problems can't seem to get unstuck, when nothing else can stop the coming storm, we still have one weapon: Our attitude. Our ability to face the storm... *and laugh.*

It would be valuable enough if keeping a positive attitude were simply a technique for avoiding depression—a mental gimmick for minimizing the doom and gloom, for looking ahead to a time when fortune might smile on us again. After all, in the normal cycle of things, bad times *do* eventually give way to good. A positive attitude at least preserves us for that brighter future.

But Spock is being even bolder. He's reminding us that good spirits can effectively *change reality now.*

For one thing, the very cells of our bodies become infused with increased vitality. And because our bodies are connected to the world, external changes are possible.

What's more, in the network of consciousness, a display of positive attitude can evoke a sympathetic reaction in other people. The resulting *communal* positivity not only creates an atmosphere for finding solutions where before none existed, but cancels out negative karma like the effect of two opposing wave forms.

If I can't control external events, I can control my attitude about them. I give up nothing by trying. I take back my life if I succeed.

11.26

What is the point of doing battle if you cannot enjoy the fruits of your victory?

LT. COMMANDER WORF: FOR THE CAUSE: Stardate Not Given

According to many traditions, "spiritual maturity" is demonstrated by an increasing ability to postpone the rewards for one's actions for longer and longer periods of time. Like the promise of "heaven", it should be enough to know that we are working steadily toward some goal, and that we'll receive the benefits *some* day.

And there's some truth to this. But the fruits of victory can't be delayed indefinitely. We are not only spiritual beings; our material dimension deserves respect. And like the Captain who knows the limitations of his crew, we must give our bodies their due—if only to reinforce positive effort and inspire ourselves to re-enter the battle.

The eventual goal may be to transcend our bodies. But in the meantime we must not pass up opportunities to "stand down" from the struggle, to consolidate recent gains and live in their afterglow; and thereby send our psyche the life-affirming message that The Path may be rocky and dangerous but the views are worth every step.

And something happens: As we become seasoned soldiers of the spirit, we find ourselves growing less and less dependent on the fruits of victory, and enjoying the struggle more and more for its own sake.

My body/mind is a gift from The Universe. I will honor its needs. I welcome new opportunities to earn the rewards which encourage my progress.

Enjoy these times... it's the time of your life that'll never come again. When it's gone... it's gone.

"SCOTTY": RELICS: 46125.3

If only we could learn the lesson before it's too late: How precious are our lives! And how fleeting is time.

The fact that we have *physical* lives makes the lesson all the more urgent. We are born, we die; and between those two events is a finite period during which we gain experience and try to achieve whatever purpose we discover for ourselves. We may not know how *long* that period is. We only know it's finite. Our death is simply the universe's reminder to *pay attention.*

Which is exactly what Scotty is trying to point out. The times we live in, the people we interact with, the very bodies through which we experience our lives—all of these are changing constantly. The precise combination of factors which are present *in this moment* will never come together again anywhere in the universe.

And so we are advised to "enjoy" these times. Not so much in the sense of "having fun", but in an attitude of *being joyful;* of seeing each moment as the unique treasure it is, and being glad for it. Of being open to each new once-in-a-lifetime opportunity for learning... and in giving thanks no matter what its lesson.

Time, like energy, can be transformed into matter. By using and appreciating the time I am given, time no longer "passes". It becomes part of me.

11.28

We all work for our supper. You'll be surprised how much sweeter it tastes when you do.

ALEXIS: PARADISE: Stardate Not Given

We take so much for granted. We accept the ease and comfort our technology gives us with hardly a thought.

And for the most part this is good. By not having to deal with the physical challenges our ancestors did, we are free to concentrate on more "spiritual" matters—like self-improvement, creative expression, the Quest for Truth.

But there is a price. We can become too lazy, too dependent. We can forget how to "fend for ourselves" if our technology were ever taken. We can lose touch with the most basic requirements of our own survival.

We can also lose touch with the "simple pleasures" of living. Like the satisfaction of growing the very food we put on our table. Or the pride that comes from helping to build the machines we use or the homes we inhabit. Or the delight in creating something—out of words, or clay, or sound—for our own personal enjoyment.

Often, our recurring feelings of being "unfulfilled" are simply the result of having too few opportunities to practice self-reliance, to do things for ourselves. To "work for our supper".

Fortunately, it's a situation that's easily remedied.

I will endeavor to link what I do with the benefits I enjoy. I will find projects or hobbies that allow me to "taste" the fruits of my own labor.

*Try to maintain your emotional equanimity.
You should not be concerned with
success or failure.*

LIEUTENANT TUVOK: COLD FIRE: Stardate Not Given

"Equanimity" is simply Tuvok's ten-credit word for "emotional balance". It's the opposite of all those wild mood swings many of us give ourselves—from agony to ecstacy, depression to exhilaration, fear to fearlessness. And make no mistake: We *do* give them to ourselves. Because heightened emotions can become the drug we use to mask our own lack of direction. We may not feel a sense of purpose, but at least we feel *alive,* right?

The problem is, it's a terrible price to pay. If our emotional roller-coaster rides don't harm our bodies, they *will* damage our relationships.

One of the best ways to regain emotional balance is to detach ourselves from the outcome of our efforts. Not that we shouldn't have goals, or strive to achieve them. It's just that, while we're "striving", worrying about whether we'll succeed or fail can distract us. By *not* being concerned with success, we free ourselves to concentrate on *the job itself,* and on doing the best we can.

And that frees The Universe to do the job *It* does best: Balancing our wants with what we need in order to grow.

Which is the *spiritual* version of equanimity.

*I can feel alive without using my emotions as
a thrill ride. I will control my temperment and my
own effort, and let The Universe control the rest.*

11.30

Rudeness will get you nowhere.

QUARK: FOR THE CAUSE: Stardate Not Given

A lesson in social graces... from *Quark*—?

Even Quark has standards for "appropriate behavior", though they're often at odds with other cultures. One area of agreement, however, is that social interactions are *not* the proper context for venting one's frustrations.

But that is frequently just what we do. We bring our unresolved personal issues from one situation into the next. Angry over our jobs or relationships or unmet personal goals, we end up "taking it out" on others—including people we don't even know.

Make that *"Especially* people we don't even know."

Those who work in the public sector, like Quark, encounter this phenomenon daily. From bartenders to sales clerks, the "anonymous" people we meet in stores and public facilities make easy targets for our unhappiness. Since we have no relationship to lose, we somehow feel under no obligation to treat them with courtesy. But *they* are required to treat *us* with courtesy or else we report them to their superiors (which gives us back the sense of power we evidently lost in some previous situation).

It's not just that these people deserve better from us. It's that practicing courtesy—*especially on people we don't even know*—is a good indicator of spiritual growth.

The person most affected by my rudeness—or my kindness—is me. My first reaction to frustration is to be even more respectful and courteous to others.

SECTOR

CORRESPONDING TO THE TERRAN MONTH OF
December

That *is the exploration that awaits you: Not mapping stars and studying nebulae, but charting the unknown possibilities of existence.*

Q : ALL GOOD THINGS...: 47988

No matter how far we may go on our travels among the galaxies, we are never more than a heartbeat from the primary object of our explorations: *Us.*

Q knew what we only suspected. Stars, nebulae, and alien lifeforms were never really the point. Bringing back new information about the cosmos, or new technology and artifacts from other civilizations—even forming new alliances—are only by-products of The Real Adventure.

Because in pushing the boundaries of the known universe, we are actually expanding the limits of our own minds. In journeying through space and time, we are really charting the hidden dimensions within *us.* By mapping stars and the routes between them, we are not only connecting with one another but to Existence itself.

Many of us remain blissfully unaware that our explorations "out there" are only symbols of this inner quest. And maybe that's as it should be, for then we can enjoy the adventure for its own sake. But someday, when we look back, we'll see that we haven't so much been on a voyage through the universe, as into our selves.

Today offers a new opportunity to explore my self. With each new task I redefine Who I Am. With every new challenge I transform my life for the better.

12.2

Our feelings are what make us all human.

COMMANDER RIKER: THE ICARUS FACTOR: 42686.4

Naturally, the Commander doesn't mean "human" in the sense of a particular species from Terra. He's talking about the one personal quality shared by living, sentient beings everywhere: The ability to *feel*.

But it's more than a mere sensitivity to physical stimuli. All life forms can sense and respond to the external environment. "Feelings" refers to an *interior* sensitivity. And what's being felt is one's own state of mind.

The problem is, many of us are *so* sensitive to this inner feedback that we've come to fear it—often to the point of more or less disconnecting ourselves from it. Ironically, the very people who show *no* feelings are sometimes the ones who feel *most deeply.* Or at least they could in the past—before some emotional trauma hurt them badly enough that their mind created a shield to prevent any further assaults.

Yet that reaction, too, is "human". So we must not only be aware of our own tendency to "raise shields", we must recognize how *others* may be cut off from their deeper feelings. In that recognition, we begin to humanize them. Which eventually leads to forgiving them. Which in turn rehumanizes *us,* and reminds us to forgive ourselves.

If my own feelings make me defensive, so it must be with others. Today I will lower my "shields", so that someone else will feel safe in lowering theirs.

Why is any object we don't understand always called a 'thing'?

DR. McCOY: STAR TREK/TM: 7412

Here's the harsh truth right up front: The words we use to "name" an object convey as much about *us* as the object itself. Maybe more.

Other people, for instance. Whole races have been reduced to their skin colors or prominent features. Members of a particular sex are labeled by a single "function" or physical characteristic rather than by their individual qualities or proper names. This is done (supposedly) because we don't yet *know* their qualities or names. Unfortunately, by sticking people into these simplistic boxes, we can prevent ourselves from *ever* knowing them as unique individuals. They remain mere objects to us; and we thereby remain simplistic and insensitive.

And if we can turn *people* into objects, how much less consideration we give the natural world! Animals, plants, land—whole planets—are "things" to possess and exploit. Which defines *us* as tyrants and exploiters.

"Thing" is a perfectly good word, a useful word. It points. It acknowledges existence. It "stands for" objects until we get to know them better. But in doing so it points to our ignorance. It reminds us that we don't understand.

Ideally, it reminds us to *keep learning.*

My words describe me as much as the objects they represent. I will listen for what they teach me about myself, and learn another key to my transformation.

12.4

Patience is a lost virtue to most. To me, an ally.

ODO: NECESSARY EVIL: 47282.5

In a world of warp-drives and personal transporters, time is perceived differently. The rhythms of biology are no longer our primary reference. Our "natural" sense of time is redefined by the increasing speed of our artifical devices. Patience is a lost virtue if only because our inter-actions with technology rarely require it!

But our *personal* interactions are another matter. Here, biology is still the defining factor. "Real time" must be readjusted for the slower pace of thinking and feeling; for the deliberate nurturing of relationships; and for the subtle, cumulative effects which combine to change our lives. One spiritual tradition symbolizes this "living" pro-cess in the sacred image of the lotus flower, unfolding itself petal by petal until it is finally revealed in all its glory.

Patience is the quiet acceptance of the fact that some things must be allowed, like the lotus, to unfold at their own pace. Love is the classic example. Likewise develop-ing a spiritual discipline, overcoming our fears, or finding our life's purpose. These things must "unfold". Rushing them can only disrupt (or prevent) their flowering.

In the process, it's not really patience that becomes our ally. It's *The Universe*.

I won't be rushed by the timetable of technology. I will take time to fully absorb the lessons I must learn. My life is unfolding at just the right pace.

If an event were important enough to be recovered, why would it be forgotten?

DATA: VIOLATIONS: 45429.3

Like many quirks of being human—or at least being *sentient*—our tendency to forget events in the past (and then remember/recover them) is difficult to understand. Why *do* we forget things that may be critical to our mental health or personal growth? Why must we forget *at all?*

Actually, unless there are organic factors, memories of past events are never forgotten completely. Our minds simply place certain memories beyond the reach of our consciousness. Recovery is temporarily "disallowed".

Not that those memories don't continue to affect us. Our subconscious often draws on suppressed memories to make its decisions—or give us hunches. Our attitudes toward other people and toward the world may be influenced by such memories as well. Often profoundly.

Whatever the case, we can trust that something *purposeful* is going on. Some memories, for example, may elude us until we're better equipped to deal with them emotionally. Or until we have more information, or more experience, or more patience. Sometimes *not remembering* is simply meant to trigger the very question Data asks.

And in searching for the answer, we may learn something about ourselves we would never know otherwise.

My forgetting is as purposeful as my remembering. If a memory is blocked, I will ask "why", and open myself to what The Universe wants to teach me.

12.6

There can be no justice as long as there are absolutes. Even life itself is an exercise in exceptions.

CAPTAIN PICARD : JUSTICE : 41255.6

Let's start with the physical world:

Most of us have learned that the universe is founded on certain invariable laws. In every place we've yet explored, these laws seem to hold, to the point that we call them "absolutes". If there are occasional exceptions, it's only because some "higher" law has intervened—a law we may not have fully understood, or even knew existed.

Science continually attempts to account for the interactions between all these laws/absolutes. And if the result is summarized in a statement which says something like "A equals B + C, except on Tuesdays", that statement is no less an absolute for including an "exception".

So how does all this apply to the concept of justice?

For one thing it should make us more humble, more *careful*. Are we sure our "laws"—that is, our attempts to apply the scientific model to social interactions—shouldn't allow for exceptions? Do our laws of "justice" try to enforce a level of certainty and inflexibility that doesn't even exist in the physical world? And are there any "higher" laws which can occasionally intervene?

"An eye for an eye" is one law. "Forgive your enemies" is another. Which is the higher one? In every case—?

As I judge, so will I be judged. As I define "justice" for others, so will "justice" be applied to me.

Just give up—? I don't think so!

DR. BASHIR : DISTANT VOICES : Stardate Not Given

There's no better formula for success: In striving to achieve our goals, we should never give up. In following our dreams, we mustn't give up. In seeking to transform ourselves, we simply *cannot* give up.

The age-old wisdom about success consisting of one part inspiration and 99 parts perspiration is true. It's not intellectual brilliance that ultimately wins out. It's not our good looks. It's not our talent, or money, or even who we know that is most likely to bring success.

It's our willingness to *keep trying,* to stay in the game, to embrace the ongoing struggle. Even more, it's the realization that achieving our goals and dreams isn't the top priority anyway. These are just excuses to continue refining our *character*—to make us more committed, more courageous individuals; to force us to look within ourselves, to connect with the deeper resources each of us has, but we pretend we can get along without.

Few of us will make these life-enriching connections unless we are confronted by some extraordinary threat or challenge. Ironically, it is when we feel defeated by these events, when we are tempted to "just give up", that we are most able to discover and release our true power.

Be still. Try to feel it, *live* it. Don't give up until you *do.*

I may not achieve all my goals and dreams. But I will achieve something even greater by continuing to make the effort, by not giving up.

12.8

I admire gall!

LIEUTENANT WORF : THE SURVIVORS : 43152.4

The omnipedia on the Ship's Computer defines "gall" as "…rudeness; impudence; asserting oneself in a way which ignores authority, custom or convention."

Which is why gall is usually considered a negative personal trait in "polite society". But it can be decidedly *positive* in situations where taking risks is necessary to the achievement of one's goals. Including spiritual ones.

Because among the traits that usually accompany gall is a healthy dose of confidence (bordering on *over*-confidence), as well as a readiness to take a stand for what one believes—even when doing so would invite danger. Klingons call this kind of brazen self-assertion "nuQ'nuH", while Terrans know it as "chutzpah".

We should all be so brazen. And the fact is, we *can* be. When it comes to asserting ourselves for what we believe, we never face the danger alone anyway. Inspired by our example, others will join us. And since the energies of the universe are drawn to efforts that complement its own redemptive purposes, we have all the support we need.

Try this exercise for developing your own capacity for "gall". Without putting anyone else at risk, do something that flies in the face of convention, or goes against "the odds". Savor what it feels like. Notice how you survive, win or lose. Do it again. Someday it will matter.

I am confident. The Universe is with me. I take risks for what I believe in, and for my spiritual growth.

No one can guarantee the actions of another.

SPOCK: THE DAY OF THE DOVE: Stardate Not Given

There's a saying common to dozens of planetary cultures: "Speak for yourself." Because as much as we may *think* we know someone else, we can never presume to express exactly what they feel or think.

The same goes for "guaranteeing" another person's actions. After all, we don't live inside their minds. We can't feel what they feel, remember their memories, know every little detail that might affect their behavior.

We have a hard enough time knowing what makes *us* tick. How many times have we surprised ourselves— positively *and* negatively—by doing something we never thought we could (or *would*) do?

When we pretend to know someone else better than we have a right, it's often an expression of our desire to know our*selves* better. After all, we'd like to be able to count on *some*body. We desperately want *some*one to be reliable, consistent... *knowable.* And when we fail our own test, we may transfer those hopes to someone else.

There's another saying that's almost universal: "Know thyself." The good news is, *we can.* By being objective about our own behavior. By running the daily diagnostic on ourselves called "meditation".

My first priority is guaranteeing my own actions. As I become aware of my behavior, I can begin to change it for the better. On that I can depend.

12.10

Life is full of surprises.

GARAK: THE SEARCH, PART II: Stardate Not Given

We shouldn't be surprised at being surprised.

Life is rarely predictable. Nor would we *want* it to be. Our lives tend to melt into nothingness when things no longer surprise us. An unvarying routine can literally sap our strength and strangle our minds. We begin to sleep-walk through life, shrivel up spiritually.

In contrast, we often feel most alive when we don't know what's going to happen next. The only thing we *do* know is that challenges lie ahead, events we can't even foresee are bound to change our lives; and if we don't pay attention, we may learn our next lesson the hard way.

And that's precisely the point: The Universe is still in control, still teaching us its lessons. In fact, surprise is sometimes the best way to focus our attention on the most important ones. If we weren't caught by surprise now and then, we might go on ignoring some crucial fact, some new experience necessary for our continued growth. Surprise is the "wake-up call", the knock at the door, the bell ringing for our next class.

If we don't think we're ready, we aren't giving ourselves enough credit.

I am thankful for the surprises in my life, pleasant or otherwise. I know The Universe is using them to point to areas in my life that need attention.

Even the eagle knows when to sleep.

COMMANDER CHAKOTAY: RESOLUTIONS: 49690.1

It's a common reaction: When at last we demonstrate some small measure of mastery over our own lives, we often feel an even greater need to prove ourselves. When we finally assume command over our personal circumstances—which is what the eagle represents—we also assume the role of "spiritual example" for others.

And it's almost like we take on a new job. *We* are now "the strong one". *We* must be the role model. Others begin looking to us for advice, reassurance, inspiration. Having shown a glimmer of our divine spark, it has now become *our* responsibility to lead the way. If not save the world.

Part of this messianic attitude comes from the understandable desire to confirm that we really *have* seen The Light, that our newly-acquired spiritual gifts are for real and not some fluke. The problem is, we are still fallible, vulnerable, imperfect creatures. We can't be round-the-clock role models. That's far too much pressure.

Besides which we still have our *own* personal needs. For advice and reassurance. For room to experiment, to make mistakes without feeling like we're causing others to stumble. For simply being alone now and then.

Part of spiritual mastery is knowing when to put our messianic self-image to bed and just *be ourselves.*

No matter how spiritually "adept" I become, I am still the same person. Though I soar like the eagle, I share the same basic needs as everyone else.

12.12

Without trust there's no friendship, no closeness... none of the emotional bonds that make us who we are.

COMMANDER RIKER: LEGACY: 44215.3

The concept almost seems self-contradictory: To form a bond of such closeness, such intimacy, that two people feel connected even when they're apart; yet which leaves each free and unrestricted by the other.

And it *would* be contradictory—without mutual trust.

Trying to *enforce* closeness is the real contradiction. Because if we insist on knowing where someone else is and what they're doing whenever we're separated, we only drive them away. If we insist on being "alike" as a sign of our affection—the same beliefs, the same interests, the same social circles—we create a relationship based on meeting requirements, not on *being ourselves*. It's still a "relationship", but it can't be as close.

Trust is our gift of freedom for others to be who they are, to go where they may, and to return to us of their own free will. To trust others in this way is really to value our-*selves,* to believe that we are *worth* returning to—ironically, even if the other person ends up *not* returning!

The emotions that build around these trusting, voluntary relationships invite us to grow, to accept, to *be*. They expand our feeling of connection to others, and therefore extend the boundaries of our Self.

I am truly connected to others only as I free them to be who they are, and free myself to be who I am.

> *All the knowledge of the universe, and all the power that it bestows, is of intrinsic value to everyone.*
>
> JETREL : JETREL : 48832.1

As Captain Picard has said on more than one occasion, "The search for knowledge is always our primary mission." Here, Jetrel is simply trying to explain *why.*

Why should knowledge be so all-important? After all, isn't there something to be said for the bliss of ignorance? Besides, who wouldn't trade a few I.Q. points—or a few gigabytes of cerebral storage space—for an increased ability to enjoy life? Or a greater sense of purpose? Or to feel more *loved*? Aren't these things far more valuable to us than the mere accumulation of facts?

Jetrel's point is that "knowing" *is the key* to increasing our enjoyment of life. Knowledge is what gives us the ability to discover and act out our life's purpose. To know the universe, to know someone else, to know our*selves*— as fully as we can—*is* to feel more loved. And to love.

Knowledge doesn't only bestow power. It bestows the power for *good.* It also bestows the recognition that we must use that power to increase everyone's good.

Everyone's. Because if we hoard our knowledge, if we try to use it solely for our own advantage, it quickly loses its value. In fact, it eventually turns on us.

As I make new discoveries about myself and the universe, I will look for opportunities to share my knowledge with others, and for them to share theirs.

12.14

A good joke just seems to make fear dissolve.

NEELIX: THE THAW: Stardate Not Given

Often true. In fact, even a *bad* joke (which Neelix was known for) can do the job. The question is, *why?*

In the midst of a crisis, most of us have a tendency to focus so intently on our problem that we lose sight of everything else. And fortunately so, since this ability enables us to devote all our energies to finding a solution.

But sometimes our fears have no identifiable source; there is no specific problem to solve. We simply harbor a vague, seemingly-permanent sense of foreboding.

It is *not* permanent. And that's precisely what a joke— or some other distraction—can show us.

By giving us something else to focus on, we step back from our fears for the moment. By the release of tension a good laugh (or even a *forced* laugh) can give us, we extract ourselves from our emotional straitjacket. In that moment, we recognize that *we can control our attitude,* even if we can't control the situation.

Better yet, we eventually discover that, by controlling our attitude, we *do* control the situation. Detached from our fears, we regain our perspective, clarity of mind. We reconnect with our inner, healing resources. We remember that, with The Universe, all things are possible.

I can use humor to break through fear. By giving myself opportunities to laugh as I would give myself medicine, I restore balance and perspective.

*I don't think we can start second guessing
ourselves. I think we have to proceed
normally and deal with each situation
as it occurs.*

COUNSELOR TROI : ALL GOOD THINGS… : 47988

There's something to be said for "hunches".

Despite the Vulcan preference for logic, the rest of us rarely make decisions by conscious thought alone. Our subconscious plays a major role—or perhaps *the* major role—processing far more data than our "aware mind" could ever gather, much less keep track of.

Unfortunately, the subconscious decisions (hunches) presented to our awareness often seem too easy. We become suspicious of the fact that we didn't have to think very hard, or do a lot of preliminary analysis. So our logical mind begins reviewing the process and, naturally, can't always determine the basis for the decision. A second decision is made, now labeled a "guess" because we're so confused. Which is usually a big mistake.

The exception is when we realize that our first hunch is based not on our intuitive decision-making powers, but on some knee-jerk reaction or habit. Or our hormones.

Ultimately it's a matter of looking at the *source* of our decision, not the decision itself. It's a matter of learning to trust a part of ourselves we don't consciously control.

*I can feel my decisions are "right" without always
knowing how I arrived at them. I will trust my inner
guidance, and let my experience confirm the results.*

12.16

If we're going to do it, we're going to do it by the book.

CAPTAIN KIRK: THE FINAL FRONTIER: 8454

"Anything worth doing," an old proverb goes, "is worth doing *well.*" And for everything worth doing, we might add, there's probably a dozen books telling you *how.*

Doing something "by the book" is simply another way of saying, "Let's do this task/project/assignment as well as we can—according to the most reliable, time-tested information we can find." This does not mean blindly following directions. It *does* mean admitting that most of the paths we walk were explored by others before us. How foolish we would be to ignore the roadmaps they've left behind, or pass up any ships' logs that might make our own voyages safer and more productive.

And yet that is often exactly what we do. Simply because other books—or traditions or religions—were written in another cultural setting or an earlier time, we assume they can't possibly teach us anything useful. Which is like saying that anyone speaking a foreign language doesn't have anything meaningful to tell us.

We might think of "The Book" as the accumulated wisdom of past generations—the collective resources which can tell us not only what works, but how to find answers for ourselves if the existing ones *don't* work. And that's when we become authors for the *next* generation.

I am grateful for the Book of Life others have left for me. I will strive to make my own contribution.

There's always a choice.

MAJOR KIRA: INDISCRETION: Stardate Not Given

Such an easy excuse: "But I had no choice!"

Yet almost without exception, whenever we make this claim, what we're *really* saying is that we didn't like the alternatives. Or that anyone *else* would have done the same thing *we* did. Or that our decision was dictated by habit, or culture, or "nature". It was... *automatic.*

The Spiritual Path, however, is designed to make us *conscious* of what was once automatic. After all, we can't take control of what we do thoughtlessly, without even being aware of the process. First awareness, then control.

Not that we always *should* take control. If we had to think about taking every breath, if we had to consciously *tell* our hearts to beat, most of us would be fertilizer by now. There are some things better done *for* us than *by* us.

But making the choices that affect our lives, that help define the kind of people we are, are not among those things. In fact the really *tough* choices—the ones some of us would most like to hand over to someone else—are often the opportunities The Universe gives us to transform Who We Are. The times we *think* we have no choice are the very times our power to choose can blossom.

The Spiritual Path can help. Be still. Open yourself to The Infinite. You may lose count of the possibilities!

As I connect with my Source, I open myself to new directions, new alternatives, new choices.

12.18

It's the differences that have made us strong.

CAPTAIN PICARD: UP THE LONG LADDER: 42823.2

At its best, the Federation has been a grand experiment in learning to live and work together productively—despite a stunning diversity of races and cultures. In stark contrast are the nations, past and present, where "ethnic purity" is the ideal. Or where diverse cultures have tolerated one another only because of an enforced "peace".

Not that the Federation's experiment has been altogether peaceful either. Living with differences requires work. Communities must always guard against the kinds of acts which incite division. Individuals must remind themselves (and each other) how much richer the social fabric is when the whole spectrum of colors is woven in.

A community's strength, like the concept of teamwork, relies on differences, not on sameness. What one person can't do, another *can*. The experience and strength of one individual is multiplied by every other.

This principle is valid at every level, right down to our own personal lives. Because within each of us is a similar spectrum of roles and responsibilities, needs and wants, strengths and weaknesses—some of which conflict with each other. Our happiness depends not on suppressing this inner diversity, but accepting and integrating it.

I accept the diversity within me, as I do the diversity around me. I celebrate the many relationships and inner resources that are my strength.

12.19

Kind of exciting, isn't it? We just don't know!

RO LAREN : CONUNDRUM : 45494.2

Most of us feel more comfortable when things are settled. We like our problems solved, investigations completed, mysteries explained. It's nice to have a good puzzle to work on now and then. But we seem *driven* to put the pieces together so we can get on with our lives.

And yet there's a sense in which *not* settling everything is good for us. To think we know it all, or that we can solve all the big questions, is to presume we're larger than Life, to rank ourselves equal to The Universe. To recognize mystery—in fact to *celebrate* it—is to accept our place in the Scheme of Things.

Which isn't so bad. How boring life would be if there were no challenges left, nothing more for us to learn. The "Hell" envisioned by many primitive religions, in which sinners are subjected to eternal physical torment, is child's play (not to mention child*ish*) compared to the condition in which the universe holds no more secrets, in which life can no longer surprise us.

To realize that there is always something more to learn, some facet of ourselves to explore, some conundrum to unravel, keeps us energized, excited... *alive!*

And humble.

I celebrate the Mystery of existence. I give thanks for the work The Universe holds in store for me, no matter how much I've already accomplished.

12.20

After a time, you may find that "having" is not so pleasing as "wanting". It is not logical, but it is often true.

SPOCK: AMOK TIME: 3372.7

The Vulcan saying is much like the ancient Terran one: "Restrain your dreams, lest they all come true."

Yet ironically, many of us would rather hold on to our dreams than the realities they are designed to mold themselves into. After all, we can still *control* our dreams. We can eliminate whatever we don't like with a wave of our imaginations. The fantasies we have about the perfect relationship or the ideal job are "perfect" and "ideal" only because we tend to gloss over the hard work they will inevitably require. "Wanting" demands little energy. "Having" comes with lots of strings attached.

Then again, "wanting" does *project* energy. And the universe responds by coalescing its forces around our wants, and finally bringing us the realities they represent.

When we find those realities to be unfulfilling (or even self-destructive), The Universe is probably trying to teach us a lesson. It may be asking us to take responsibility for our thoughts as well as our actions. Or it may be encouraging us to look at our motivations for "wanting". Do we really *need* the things we want? Do we desire some things only because someone *tells* us we should?

Our dreams are mirrors of ourselves. Look hard.

I will dream not so much to have whatever I want, but to want what I already have.

You have no idea what the consequences might be once you involve yourself.

CAPTAIN JANEWAY: TIME AND AGAIN: Stardate Not Given

It's a worthy goal, as Tuvoc says, to "be prepared for anything." But as Janeway reminds us, we never *can* be. The smallest detail, overlooked, can ruin our best-laid plans. And even if everything *does* go "according to plan", the full effects of our actions may not be felt for weeks or years. Or generations.

Which doesn't mean we shouldn't act at all. Nor is it simply an appeal for extra caution, or still more pre-planning. For one thing, we may not have that luxury.

What it means is getting used to *not knowing*—of being able to move forward despite limited information, despite our fears and doubts. And for that we *can* prepare.

We can prepare by actively seeking "experience", by looking for new challenges where the unexpected can be expected. Naturally, we'll want to start with assignments that can't hurt us too badly if things go wrong. But just by putting ourselves in these situations, we automatically learn crucial lessons: That we *will* survive; that there is a "knowing" below the level of consciousness that can guide us; that if we take the leap, if we *do* "involve ourselves" in good faith, The Universe will respond in kind.

And then we'll not only survive; the consequences may turn out better than we could ever have dreamed!

I am never, ever alone. I receive divine guidance as I open myself to the full resources of The Universe.

12.22

...I've always believed that what you get when you love someone is greater than what you risk.

COMMANDER CHAKOTAY: TWISTED : Stardate Not Given

Chakotay tells us exactly what's "at risk" in a comment that leads up to this one. "Nothing makes us more vulnerable," he says, "than when we love someone."

Being vulnerable: That's the risk. It's also what scares us. Because to love someone is, in a sense, to give away control. Since we've allowed someone else's welfare to become as important as our own, we can now be affected by what happens to *them,* not only to us.

And it's not just what *happens;* it's what they *do.* Their every word, every act, has double the effect. An affectionate touch can send us into warp. An angry glance can jolt us like a phaser set to stun. Is the ride really worth it?

Yes. For one thing, to explore the depths of feeling we are capable of is to know ourselves better. For another, we learn a greater compassion for others, because *every*one struggles with these same issues. Even Vulcans.

Our vulnerability is also one of the few portals through which we can link with the larger Web of Life. In order to open ourselves to its riches we must lower our shields, let go of our insistence on "total control". In order to feel *its* transforming Love, we must first feel love for another.

How I love others reflects the extent to which I allow The Universe to love me. To love is to release my Higher Power and access the infinite reservoir within.

The king who would be man!

Q : DEJA Q : 43539

The sting of Q's remark depends on our awareness of a centuries-old story entitled, *The Man Who Would Be King*. The tale cautions us against our tendency to presume we know what's best for everyone, and if only the world would do as we decreed, life would be perfect.

Except that we often don't have a clue what's best for our*selves,* much less anyone else. And if everyone were to do exactly what we told them to, the world would probably be in much worse shape than it is already.

In other words, let's not appoint ourselves king, when we're really cut out to be humble peasants.

Of course, it's one thing to be humble, and another to ignore (or even deny) the royal qualities we do possess. Too often we accept the role of peasant—"man", in Q's hierarchy—when *we are capable of so much more.*

After the liberation of his country, a great Terran leader rephrased it this way: "Your playing small doesn't serve the world. There's nothing enlightened about shrinking so that other people won't feel insecure around you. We were born to manifest the glory of God within us… And as we let our own light shine, we unconsciously give other people permission to do the same."

The true king shows others the king within themselves.

I accept the awesome power within me to create and transform my own life's circumstances, and thereby demonstrate how others can do the same.

12.24

What the future holds no one knows. But forward we look, and forward we go.

COMMANDER RIKER : SECOND CHANCES : 46920.1

There is no going back. We can't undo what was done, nor can we live in the past. Why would we *want* to?

Past glories and golden eras seem even more glorious in retrospect. We lose touch with the daily struggles and concerns that made life as much of a challenge then as it is now. The mistakes we made, the wrong decisions, were not without purpose, not without their lessons. Our present is the diploma we receive for all that we've been through in the past. Do we really want to go back to kindergarten and re-learn what we already know?

Armed with all that hard-won knowledge, we can now affect and transform our future for the better. But only if we can see it coming. Only if we're looking forward.

It is still full of unknowns, yes. But that is what's so exciting. The future is not predestined. Every decision, every action, shapes it. The quality of our future lives, the character of the person we will become, is in our hands.

We cannot change the past, but we can redeem it by what we create now. This is what spiritual traditions envision (by various names) as The Messianic Age. But it is not some far distant future; it is *our* future. And the Messiah isn't coming. He is here *now,* in *us.*

I am part of the Cosmic Plan to shape the future.
My first responsibility is my own future, my own life.
If I succeed there, the rest will fall into place.

The channels are open and you are tied in.

LIEUTENANT UHURA: THE ENTERPRISE INCIDENT: 5027.4

A more profound statement of spiritual Truth was never spoken. Because the same Source that created the physical universe, that created all life—that created each of *us*—remains connected to us in ways we've only begun to imagine. One ancient Terran tradition described that Source as being "closer to us than our jugular vein." Another explains that we are sons and daughters of The Creator, embraced like a beloved child in a parent's arms.

Some traditions go even further: We are literally gods-in-the-making, sentient beings whose present form is like the caterpillar to the butterfly, the hatchling to the eagle. We are destined to soar. We may need help in learning *how,* but we certainly don't need to ask whether we *may.*

In fact, according to every one of these traditions, we have not only received divine "permission", but all the help we need. Channels to the deepest resources of The Universe are already open, or at least built into the fabric of Reality and awaiting our discovery. Better yet, discovering and *using* those channels requires no outside agency, no additional equipment. We are "tied in" by virtue of our consciousness, empowered by an inner Spirit that is the very incarnation of universal, creative energy.

With that energy we can transform ourselves and our world. And we begin simply by saying "Yes" to it.

I say "Yes!" to the power within me; "Yes!" to my connection with The Universe and everything in it!

12.26

You'll learn to build for yourselves, think for yourselves. And what you create is yours. It's what we call freedom.

CAPTAIN KIRK: THE APPLE: 3715.0

The dictionary definition is fine for political debate and historical analysis. But freedom, in a personal sense, gets down to this: *Taking responsibility for your own life.*

It begins with the commitment not to blame anyone else for the condition you're in. Others may have contributed, yes; but what you do about it now is *your* decision. Whether you continue to wallow in misery, or face your challenges with a positive attitude, is up to you. To repeat Kirk's words, what you create from your life *is yours.*

Of course, the struggle for freedom is not entirely an inner one. There are always external forces of the kind politicians and historians discuss. From a spiritual point of view, however, outward conditions exist precisely to help us bring our *inner* conditions into better focus. Our material situation represents our own spiritual harmony, or lack of it—or perhaps the spiritual obstacles we need to overcome before we can achieve it.

We may not *like* the thought that the obstacles in our lives reflect something inside us. It's easier to place the blame elsewhere. But *that's* the slave mentality that keeps us where we are. The alternative is freedom.

I accept the hard work that freedom requires. I declare my independence from old habits and restrictive beliefs. I am the architect of my own life.

A structure cannot stand without a foundation.

LIEUTENANT TUVOK: FLASHBACK: 50126.4

This is the bottom line. This is what we've been searching for—or trying to hang on to, patch up, or improve on: A foundation on which we can structure our lives.

There are parables in every spiritual tradition about the dangers of building on shifting sands, about the need for something solid to support us. Rock, the ideal foundation, symbolizes the things we can depend on, that don't change, that withstand the test of time. It's not surprising that the disciple of a certain Terran Master was renamed *Petros* (meaning "rock") when he founded what became one of the galaxy's leading spiritual institutions.

Not that an *institution* can serve as a foundation. Our foundation must be made up of the same truths that the universe itself is built on. These are the truths that institutions and traditions can only conceptualize in various ways, then show us how they apply in our daily lives.

Our task is to get down to the original bedrock, with help from those institutions and traditions—or through any *other* resource we may discover, not the least of which is that Piece-of-the-Rock buried within each of us.

And the miracle is, once we have that foundation, the structure on top practically builds itself.

I am restructuring my life, day by day, on the principles I am now learning. As I go boldly on my Spiritual Path, I anchor myself on Universal Truth.

12.28

The future contains wonders you can't even imagine. The universe could be your playground.

Q: TRUE Q: 46192.3

Though he wouldn't be called "religious" in any traditional sense, *Q* is nevertheless talking about faith.

Because he's talking about our world-view here. He's referring to the way we look at what's going on around us, the level of excitement and joy we bring to each new day, the way our hopes for the future affect our lives *now*.

He's reminding us, in so many words, that too many of us seem to wear blinders through life. We focus on our daily chores, hardly taking notice of other events or other people unless they bump into us. We lose sight of future possibilities. We lose touch with our imagination. It's almost as if, in trying to "fit" into this world, we end up *blending* into it. Like the Borg, we become "assimilated".

Q suggests a different point of view: *Don't* be assimilated. Instead, we must look on this world as if we're tourists from another dimension, scientists on holiday, seeking answers to the riddles of this strange new existence by exploring everything, questioning everything. The best way to do this, of course, is to take on the identity of one of its residents—even as we remember who we *really* are.

Maybe *Q*'s suggestion is more than it seems.

I've waited long, studied hard, and now I can go out and play! I must play fair, and take care of my playground, but I can do anything else I want!

I can only hope that the future holds even greater challenges.

COMMANDER SISKO: THE ADVERSARY: 48959.5

If we pause to consider the past year, or the past *five* years, chances are we'll be astounded at how far we've come. We've learned, we've grown. We are changed people. Most of our changes have been for the better.

What's better about us is no accident. Because it's not from having won the Telosian lottery. Or because some genie granted our wish. Most of our progress was *earned*.

And most of *that* came from being challenged.

Despite the fact that it was hard work at the time, having to overcome obstacles and climb mountains was good for us. Even the times we slipped, even when we hurt ourselves, the lessons were worth the pain.

And even if it's a cliché, hardship *does* build character. Because the stronger our opposition, the more we must learn to be creative; the more we must learn teamwork; the more we must search our souls for inner strength. It is our Adversary that brings out the Hero in us.

Which is why Sisko could plead, in all sincerity, for a future filled with even greater challenges. For only then could he—or can *we*—continue to improve.

Our challenges are gifts to grow on. We are not given more than we, with help from The Universe, can bear.

I will list three things I've learned from challenges over the past year. I will think about my biggest challenge today, and what I might learn from it.

12.30

So... five card stud, nothing wild... and the sky's the limit.

CAPTAIN PICARD: ALL GOOD THINGS…: 47988

In the Starfleet chronicles which have since become known as "The Next Generation", Captain Picard's closing words represent more than rules for a friendly game of poker. They are, in a sense, the groundrules governing The Game of Life.

For example, we agree to play the cards we're dealt. We can occasionally improve our hand, yes. But there's no switching cards with other players, or getting more cards than anybody else.

And the cards are exactly what they appear to be. A low card is a low card, not a face card. We cannot *wish* our twos into kings, our eights into aces. Nothing is "wild".

Which also means, thankfully, that the game is not arbitrary, chaotic. As much as the game may seem a matter of "luck", it is not. Astute players can develop and use *skill*—mental, spiritual, and emotional. And even though the advantage is only a few percentage points, it makes all the difference. So *much* so that, for all practical purposes, there are no limits on what we can win.

As the Captain said as he finally sat down to play, "I should've done this long ago." The good news is, there's still plenty of time for *all* of us to join the game.

I will play the "cards" I am dealt. I am holding a good hand. I'm not playing to beat the Dealer, or my fellow players, but to improve my own skills.

Those little points of light out there... the great unknown beckoning to us.

DR. BASHIR: THE QUICKENING: Stardate Not Given

Today's space voyagers weren't the first to gaze at the stars and see them as worlds like our own, complete unto themselves, teeming with other lives, other possibilities.

The writings of ancient Hindus hint at infinite worlds beyond our own, just as that tradition embraces the idea of countless lives beyond this present one—all of which are part of some grand Cosmic Plan designed to refine our souls to the point of perfection.

Points of light or points in our lives—these concepts symbolize what lies ahead for each of us. They represent a future we can only dimly imagine, yet which holds such vast possibilities that any direction opens up whole new worlds to explore, and even the faintest glimmer can illumine our Spiritual Path.

To feel the beckoning of those lights and lives is to accept the responsibility of existence. It is to acknowledge that we are ready to move ahead now, to experience new things, to learn, grow... *become.*

We have done well to come this far, through times of happiness and sadness, joy and pain, ignorance and self-discovery. All we know for sure is that there will be more of each. And that we will be better for it.

I accept the challenge of the rest of my life. The strength to move bravely and boldly into my own future is all around me, and within me.